A SIGHT SO NOBLY GRAND

MT. HOOD PARADISE PARK

A SIGHT SO NOBLY GRAND

Joel Palmer on Mount Hood in 1845

Joel Palmer

Introduction & Annotation

by

John Palmer Spencer

OREGON HISTORICAL SOCIETY
PRESS

Cover: Joel Palmer pauses at timberline during his 1845 climb on the south side of Mount Hood. The Three Sisters and Mount Jefferson rise to the south along the spine of the Cascade Range. (From an original painting by Evelyn Hicks produced specially for this publication.)

Frontis: *Paradise Park, southwest face of Mount Hood*
On the morning of 12 October, having camped in the vicinity of these alpine meadows, Palmer started up a "grassy ridge" (likely the one pictured in the left foreground) and made his way up a "cliff of snow and ice" to bypass the sheer face of Mississippi Head (pictured right). Palmer camped at Paradise Park again on the miserable night of 17 October. (OrHi 15842)

Support for the production of this special edition was generously provided by Omar C. Palmer.

Designed and produced by the Oregon Historical Society Press.

The paper used in this publication meets the minimum requirements of American National Standard for Information Sciences—Permanence of Paper for Printed Library Materials, ANSI Z39.48-1984.

CONTENTS

Joel Palmer (1810 - 1881)
(OrHi 66086)

PREFACE

OCTOBER 1845 MARKED A MILESTONE in the history of the Oregon Trail; a group of emigrants crossed the flanks of Mount Hood over the Cascade Range for the first time. One of their leaders, Joel Palmer, made the first recorded climb to the glaciated upper reaches of the mountain. This book is a day-by-day account of those historic events in Palmer's words.

The body of this special edition consists of thirty-three consecutive days of diary entries from Palmer's 1847 Oregon Trail classic, *Journal of Travels Over the Rocky Mountains*. That book grew out of the extensive notes Palmer made during his six-month trek from Laurel, Indiana to Oregon City, Oregon in 1845. With its wealth of descriptive and practical information about both the journey and the Oregon Territory, the book served as a guide for later emigrants. Several editions of the journal guided westbound travelers toward the Oregon County. In 1993, the Oregon Historical Society Press republished the journal in its entirety.

Joel Palmer, Sam Barlow, and thirty wagons traveled 130 miles around the south side of Mount Hood in 1845. Their trip represents but one month of a migration that spanned nearly six months and 2,000 miles. To read this portion of Palmer's journal is to sense that it was an unusually significant and urgent month. Indeed, it was the dramatic core and highlight of the whole journey. Omar C. "Slug" Palmer, Joel Palmer's great-great-grandson, worked to make Palmer's *Journal of Travels* accessible to a wider public. Slug's efforts and vision have made this book possible, and as his grandson, it has been my privilege and pleasure to annotate the volume.

Three years ago I hiked five miles from Timberline Lodge to Paradise Park and slept there, unaware that my ancestor Joel Palmer had camped and begun his climb on Mount Hood from that very place. This book would have been valuable to me then, and I hope it will be valuable to anyone who seeks a deeper appreciation of the mountain's past.

SEVERAL COMMENTS ARE IN ORDER regarding the format and annotation of this edition. Palmer's original *Journal of Travels* is a long narrative. I have divided the text into chapters to highlight significant turning points in Palmer's account. The footnotes are likewise my own, and are intended to clarify Palmer's route through the Mount Hood wilderness. In *Journal of Travels*, familiar geographic features are difficult to recognize and place because they lack contemporary nomenclature. Barlow Pass is known as "the low gap." The White River is simply "a stream." Using secondary literature, topographic maps, and my own explorations of the Mount Hood area, I have identified such features and retraced Palmer's route as accurately as possible, so that interested readers might be able to do the same.

John Palmer Spencer

INTRODUCTION

THE FIRST RECORDED CLIMB on Mount Hood began roughly five miles west of where Timberline Lodge now stands. There, in the early morning of 12 October 1845, Joel Palmer started trudging up the southwest side of the mountain. With great effort he scaled an icy cliff to bypass the rocky buttress Mississippi Head, and though his moccasins had worn through and exposed his feet to the ice and snow of Zigzag Glacier, he continued climbing. It is generally believed that in this nearly barefoot condition Palmer hiked past Illumination Rock and continued ascending to the southeast, toward Crater Rock, reaching an elevation of roughly 9,000 feet on the 11,235 foot peak. After a dangerous late afternoon descent across an unstable and crevassed ice field, he marched some twenty miles back to a camp on White River, arriving around eleven o'clock.

That extraordinary day is the highlight of this excerpt from Palmer's 1847 journal, and a critical moment in the history of Mount Hood. In his journal, Palmer made the first authoritative claim that the mountain could be ascended to the top. Only a decade later, in August 1857, Portland newspaperman Henry L. Pittock and three other men planted a makeshift banner on the summit celebrating the first authenticated climb to Oregon's highest point. Over the years many would follow; today Mount Hood is one of the world's most frequently climbed major peaks, perhaps second only to Fujiyama in

*The Upper Cascades of the
Columbia River*
Emigrants floating the
Columbia River encountered
these dreaded rapids forty-
five miles down river from
The Dalles. Rafts had to be
brought ashore for the arduous portage around the
white-water and, to make
matters worse for the weary
travelers, they were required
to pay a toll by the Indians
whose land they were crossing. Indeed, numerous
Indian villages were located
near the Cascades, whose
churning water made for excellent fishing.

   The Cascades (these rapids
were the source of the name
of the Cascade Range) were
submerged in 1938 under the
backed-up waters of Bonneville Dam. Ironically, geolo-
gists believe it was a natural
dam that created the rapids in the first place. About seven hundred years ago a mas-
sive landslide from Greenleaf Peak completely dammed the river—it has been sug-
gested that this was the legendary "Bridge of the Gods"—and created a lake that
stretched to present-day Umatilla in eastern Oregon. Eventually the river forced its
way through the great rock barrier, creating the Cascades Rapids.
(C.E. Watkins photo. OrHi 71175)

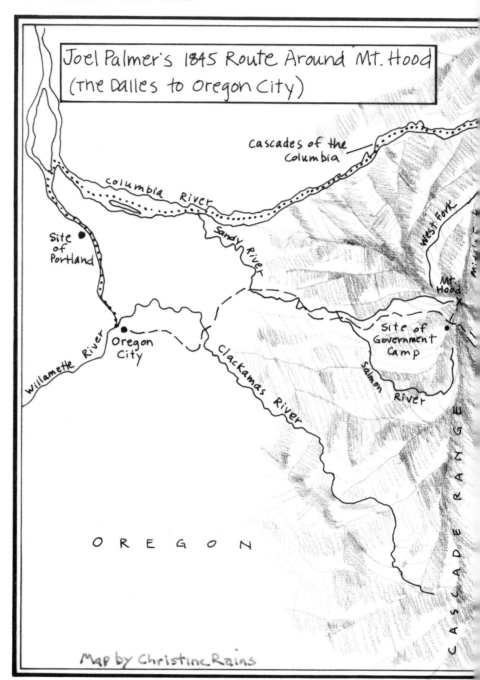

Joel Palmer's 1845 Route Around Mt. Hood
(The Dalles to Oregon City)

cascades of the Columbia

Columbia River

Sandy River

West Fork

Middle Fork

Mt. Hood X

Site of Portland

Site of Government Camp

Willamette River

Oregon City

Salmon River

Clackamas River

O R E G O N

C A S C A D E   R A N G E

Map by Christine Rains

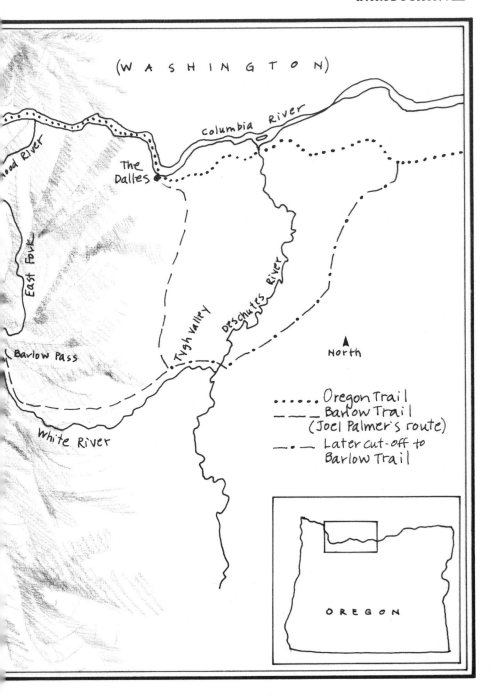

Japan. Those who flock to the mountain for skiing, hiking, and visits to world-renowned Timberline Lodge far outnumber the climbers. Indeed, a rich and compelling human history has unfolded on the slopes of Mount Hood, and much of that recorded history can be traced to the day of Joel Palmer's climb in 1845.

Though it marks the beginning of a modern era on the mountain, Palmer's ascent belongs to, and signals the closing of, an earlier age. Unlike climbers of later years—even those who approached the mountain almost immediately following him—Palmer did not ascend Mount Hood for recreation or for challenge. His purpose was utterly practical. He sought a clear view of the rugged Cascades to the south and west to determine where his train of twenty-three wagons might pass. In 1845, all that mattered was reaching "Eden" (as the emigrants sometimes thought of the Willamette Valley), before winter set in.

Mount Hood took on stark significance for the emigrants. The mountain barred the emigrants' passage into Eden; it also provided a place from which they could survey the land ahead. As with their ancestors and their contemporaries (Henry David Thoreau, Ralph Waldo Emerson, and other transcendentalists are notable exceptions), the pioneers had a fairly wary and unromantic relationship with nature. Survival was an ongoing struggle, and mountains, with their rugged terrain and unpredictable weather, were places to avoid or bypass. This reluctance would change soon.

In the decades following Palmer's journey, white emigrants settled the Oregon Country in ever-increasing numbers. As was the case throughout a nation undergoing industrialization, their relationship with the land and the mountain grew less arduous. No longer an obstacle, Mount Hood became a destination, a place from which to make a living, a place of scenery, of sport, even of spirituality.

Joel Palmer's journal of October 1845 evokes an earlier, elemental, world where several dozen families struggled on the lower slopes of a mountain, while one man climbed high to see what kind of route they might follow to safety. To read his account of the first trek across the Cascades by a wagon train is to read one of Oregon's most stirring dramas. Through it we can appreciate how our relationship with "the mountain" has changed.

A SIGHT SO NOBLY GRAND begins at The Dalles, on the Columbia River, during the third year of organized oxen-drawn wagon travel on the Oregon Trail. "No wagons," as Palmer says, "had ever gone below this place." Ahead, the

Columbia had cut its great gorge through the Cascade Mountains, leaving no suitable place for a road. Indeed, the only possible highway through this steep-walled chasm was the river itself. Emigrants dismantled their wagons, floating them on rafts down the Columbia and the Willamette to Oregon City.

They faced a different river than the one we know today. The treacherous rapids known as the "Cascades" of the Columbia were not yet drowned by the waters behind Bonneville Dam. The cascades forced emigrants ashore for the arduous task of reassembling the wagons, portaging them over a difficult road around the rough cataracts, and dismantling them again for the rest of the voyage. If blessed with favorable weather, they might continue without delay. When fierce Gorge winds whipped the river into a turbulent sea, travelers had little choice but to huddle in waiting on shore.

Palmer and his emigrant group were understandably weary by the time they reached The Dalles. Five months and 1,800 miles earlier they had "jumped off" from Independence, Missouri—then the western frontier of the United States—into the land variously known as Indian Country and the Great American Desert. They had just struggled through the steep and rocky Blue Mountains of eastern Oregon, one of the Trail's most severe obstacles. Emigrants and oxen alike had emerged from the Blues in weakened condition. The end was visibly near: for the past one-hundred-and-fifty miles, they had walked toward "the mountain" fixed on the horizon like a capstone of their journey. It must have been upsetting, indeed, to arrive at The Dalles on 29 September and discover they still faced their most serious decision.

To receive guided passage down the river, Palmer and the others would need to wait at least ten days—a costly delay, considering their scarce food and resources—and then continue only at great expense and danger. In such circumstances other emigrants had constructed makeshift rafts and relied upon their own piloting skills, often with tragic results. Palmer chose an equally dangerous alternative: to travel around the south side of Mount Hood. He and his group hoped to follow an Indian trail through the dense forests.

No wagon train had ever made such a trip. A group of seven wagons had embarked on the same journey only a few days earlier, led by Sam Barlow of Kentucky. Barlow allegedly said that, "God never made a mountain that He did not make a place for a man to go over it or under it." A week later the Kentuckian's progress seemed less promising; Palmer reports in his journal that the Barlow party had traveled twenty-five miles into the interior and found the route to be "impracticable."

Nonetheless, Palmer decided that he, too, would attempt the mountain route, and persuaded fifteen families to come along. On the first of October, twenty-three wagons left The Dalles with the intention of making "a trip over the mountains." They would try to join Barlow in his efforts.

IT WOULD PROVE TO BE the most trying stretch of the westward trek. For all of its considerable hardship and uncertainty, the Oregon Trail was, by 1845, a fairly established route. Native Americans, and later white explorers, fur traders, and missionaries had criss-crossed the Far West. Emigrants did not have to wonder, as did Lewis and Clark in 1805, where they might cross the seemingly impassable Continental Divide; South Pass in Wyoming was well traveled and, according to explorer John C. Frémont, no more formidable than a carriage ride up Washington, D.C.'s Capitol Hill. By 1845, hundreds of prairie schooner wagons had crossed the Oregon Trail, carving the ruts that remain visible today. For miles, Palmer's contingent fixed their sights on places like Fort Laramie and Fort Hall with the confidence of people who knew where they were going.

This all changed on the journey around Mount Hood. There was no road for the wagons, only a trail. The emigrants would need to clear their own way. At first, the task was manageable. Little or no work was required through the open prairie country south of The Dalles and into Tygh Valley where, on 3 October, Palmer found the wagons of the Barlow train.

In crossing the Cascades, however, the emigrants traversed the great dividing line in Oregon's climate and landscape where eastern desert separates from lush western rain forest. As they veered west into the mountains, semi-arid prairie gave way to scattered Ponderosa and yellow pine stands, which in turn would merge into a great, unbroken expanse of Douglas fir, hemlock, and spruce. At the center of this ever-thickening forest stood Mount Hood. Soaked incessantly by rain and snow, its foothills were blanketed by dense underbrush and thick timber. It was an impossible wilderness. Yet, the emigrants would try to clear their way through it, equipped only with axes and saws.

The problem was not merely how to clear the road, but *where* to clear. As a route intended for travel on foot or horseback, the Indian trail was unsuitable for the cumbersome "horse canoes" of the white travelers. There were other assumed dangers. Would the mountains spill into rocky canyons impassable to wagons and oxen? Were there raging rivers to avoid? Backtracking would be a dangerous waste of time. It was essential to get through before the onset of winter.

These concerns were the pretext for Palmer's climb of 12 October. The mountain, though such a frustrating barrier, would offer an unparalleled view of the land, and possible passes, to the south and west of it. From his high vantage point that day, Palmer saw two promising gaps, one of them passing through what is now Government Camp and down Laurel Hill—the eventual route of Barlow Road. Two days later, however, an impending storm and the approach of winter put the road clearing effort in jeopardy. In his journal, the usually optimistic Palmer sounds desperate and confused as he considers two equally untenable courses of action. They could continue, and risk getting caught between two rivers swollen by heavy rains, or they could make a long retreat back to The Dalles. He writes with the urgency of a man who feels responsible for fifteen families he has led into the wilderness.

One year later, in the winter of 1846, the Donner party would experience a similar sense of desperation. They, too, gambled on a route that had never been traveled by wagons. But they lost precious time as a result, and were besieged by a severe blizzard as they entered California's Sierra Nevadas. Their fate is grimly familiar: stopped short, and forced to encamp on the eastern fringe of the mountains' crest all winter, nearly half of the Donner party starved. Of those who survived, several did so only by eating their dead companions.

Such was not the outcome, of course, for the Oregon emigrants of 1845. Their situation, though difficult, was not as severe, and Palmer devised a sensible solution that made the best of their circumstances. Because there was no time to finish the road, they would build a makeshift cabin, "Fort Deposit," in which wagons and belongings could be stored and guarded for the winter. Most of the company would follow a wet and snowy trail to Oregon City on foot and horseback.

Still, that final push to the Willamette Valley was probably the most miserable of all their experiences on the Oregon Trail. After two weeks of torrential rains, dense fog, and snow, most of the pioneers straggled into "the settlement"—Oregon City—in cold and starving little groups. Palmer arrived on the first of November, exactly one month after his departure from The Dalles. His journal is a moving testimonial to the suffering and ultimate triumph of those final seventeen days.

There is a tendency to romanticize the pioneers, especially so in the case of the Palmer-Barlow party of 1845. They are Oregon's mythic pioneer heroes, legendary for their stamina and courage, and rightfully so. But they were lucky as well. Attempting to force thirty wagons through the Mount Hood wilderness in October was a dubious venture. It is sobering to read Palmer's account and imagine what might have happened had they, like the Donner party a year later, been caught in an unexpected snowstorm; or, had the people of Oregon City not heard of their plight and sent desperately needed provisions into the mountains. In 1845, leadership, determination, and luck carried Joel Palmer and his fellow emigrants through the Mount Hood wilderness.

AFTER THAT WINTER, the mountain would no longer be a barrier to the wagon trains of white settlers. In the spring of 1846, while Palmer went back to Indiana to fetch his family for a permanent move to Oregon (and ultimately an eventful career in Oregon politics), Sam Barlow stayed and obtained a franchise from the territorial legislature to develop the south-side route into a toll road. Construction began that spring, and was completed by July. The first wagons to travel the new Barlow Road were those left at Fort Deposit the previous winter. Later that fall more than one hundred and fifty others followed the route. Though formidable in many places—notably Laurel Hill—the new road was already replacing the Columbia River as the standard route to Oregon City.

The Barlow Road had a significant impact on Oregon's history. Emigrants poured into the territory in growing numbers, and the presence of so many U.S. citizens helped lead to statehood and the settlement of a long-standing battle with Britain for sovereignty. Judge Matthew P. Deady, a distinguished public figure in the early history of the state, claimed later that Barlow Road "contributed more towards the prosperity of the Willamette Valley and the future state of Oregon than any other achievement prior to the building of the railways in 1870." (*McNeil's Mount Hood*, p.23)

Such prosperity came at the expense of peoples who had known and revered Mount Hood and the other great Cascade volcanoes for thousands of years. It was an Indian trail that led Joel Palmer's company out of the Mount Hood wilderness when inclement weather set in. For the Pacific Northwest Indians, however, the subsequent rush of white settlers through the Cascades was a catastrophe. With the publication of Terence O'Donnell's *An Arrow in the Earth: General Joel Palmer and the Indians Of Oregon* (Oregon Historical Society Press, 1991) we now have an invaluable study of what O'Donnell terms "that five-act tragedy called the Indian Wars of Oregon." It was a tragedy that

Joel Palmer, as an early superintendent of Indian affairs in the Oregon Territory, struggled in vain to prevent.

IN THE 1850s, less than a decade after the passage around Mount Hood had been established, a few settlers began to beat a path back to the mountain, this time to ascend to its summit. In so doing, they were pioneers once again.

In the mid-nineteenth century mountaineering was not at all common. Great peaks had traditionally been feared as a domain of gods, demons, and beasts; even as recently as 1725, a published guide to Switzerland included a classification of Alpine dragons. Even without such formidable wildlife, what of terrain and weather? To venture into high-elevation wilderness was to foolishly invite disaster.

It was in the name of scientific exploration that such attitudes began to change. For countless centuries people lived in the shadow of Mont Blanc in France without leaving any written record of climbing activity. In 1760, Swiss scientist Horace Benedict de Saussure launched a campaign to climb the 15,781 foot peak—the highest in the Alps—so that he could study its glaciers. Twenty-six years later the summit was reached, and a great milestone in the early history of mountain climbing had been established.

In the 1850s, when a handful of adventurous British aristocrats turned the Alps into "Europe's playground," mountaineering came into its own as a widely recognized sport. In an eleven-year spree that culminated with a successful ascent of the "impossible" Matterhorn in 1865, climbers ascended nearly every peak in the Alps for the first time—and no longer for science or out of necessity. To stand atop a previously unclimbed peak was now a goal in itself.

That mountaineering also developed in Oregon in the 1850s may or may not be a coincidence, but it certainly is no surprise. Oregon's emigrants were, in many cases, a restless lot willing to venture into unknown terrain. Once they had completed the journey and the process of settling in, some of the emigrants turned their attention to the mountain that so dramatically dominated the horizon of their new home.

Apparently Joel Palmer wanted to be among the first to reach the top. In August 1854, nine years after he had climbed high as a matter of necessity, the former flatlander from Indiana made plans to return to the mountain. This time, presumably hoping to ascend to the summit, he arranged to join a party of six that included Thomas Dryer, the infamous founder and editor of the

Oregonian. But Palmer did not get his chance; he arrived at the designated meeting place a day late and was left behind.

Dryer went on to claim that he and two others made the first summit ascent on that outing. Using snow depths at different elevations the party calculated the height of the mountain at 18,361 feet. Three years later, in documenting their own climb to the top on 6 August 1857, a party of four men noted that Dryer's alleged summit was probably the place now called the "Crow's Nest" on the Wy'east route—a notable achievement indeed, but not the highest point on the mountain. Dryer lashed out from his editorial page at those "panting aspirants for fame" who dared to upstage him. One of them, twenty-six year old Henry L. Pittock, was his own employee at the Oregonian. Despite Dryer's outburst, history sided with the foursome of 1857.

The following decades saw many hundreds of Oregonians cover their faces with protective veils, burnt cork, or greasepaint and make the pilgrimage to the top of Mount Hood. Following in the footsteps of the Pittock party, they trudged from the Government Camp area up the relatively straightforward but laborious "south side climb," a shorter variation of which (from Timberline Lodge) is still the most popular route.

Serious enthusiasts organized themselves, founding the short-lived Alpine Club in 1887. Shortly thereafter, in 1894, 193 climbers—154 men and 39 women—convened the first meeting of the Mazamas mountaineering society on the summit. After a season of light snowfall in 1924, the Mazamas discovered a previously unknown glacier on the south side of the mountain and paid tribute to Joel Palmer by naming it after him.

Among late-nineteenth-century visitors to the mountain, a few wanted more than to sign their names in the summit register. For years, there had been talk in Portland of illuminating the mountain at the climax of the city's Fourth of July fireworks display. In 1887, following unsuccessful attempts on four previous occasions, Portlander Will Steel, who seven years later would become a founder and the first president of the Mazamas, detonated one hundred pounds of "red fire" (highly flammable lycopodium powder) at the base of what would henceforth be known as Illumination Rock. Portlanders and others throughout the Willamette Valley enjoyed a minute-long spectacle reported in newspapers across the nation.

Two years later, in 1889, Cloud Cap Inn was built high on the north side of Mount Hood, at the 6000-foot elevation. Though some worried that the permanent shelter might blow away the winter following its construction, the building endured and stimulated a rapid growth in climbing activity on the northeastern side of the mountain, notably on the still popular Cooper Spur route. In 1915, a less durable though no less remarkable structure appeared on Mount Hood: the lookout cabin built by legendary climber and guide Elijah "Lige" Coalman on the summit itself. For eighteen years, the top of Mount Hood was inhabited all summer long, and connected with the lowlands by a telephone line used in rescue operations and the reporting of forest fires. (The cabin deteriorated after it was no longer deemed necessary as a fire lookout station and over time disintegrated).

During the 1930s Oregonians most indelibly established their presence on Mount Hood. Climbers tackled the most challenging terrain on the mountain—the awesome north and west faces. Timberline Lodge and the Magic Mile chairlift were built on the other side, near Joel Palmer's base camp of 1845. The original barrier to Eden had become a recreational paradise.

IN HIS 1937 CLASSIC *Wy'east: The Mountain* (now titled *McNeil's Mount Hood*, The Zig Zag Papers, 1990), journalist and mountaineer Fred McNeil commented that Mount Hood gives us the "happy paradox of an unchanging object that never looks the same." Indeed, as a constant backdrop to the unfolding drama of Oregon history, the mountain has not changed much. Yet, we perceive it differently than Joel Palmer did in 1845. Travelers easily cross the Cascades on the Mount Hood Loop Highway. Climbers sometimes wait in line near Crater Rock before ascending to the summit on Mount Hood's south side. The nineteenth century understanding of nature is turned on its head; once considered boundless and menacing, wilderness today has the troubled image of a clearcut patchwork in need of legal protection. Palmer's world stands in shocking contrast to our own.

Still, when we read about the pioneers of 1845 struggling to survive the mountain, we might recognize what is familiar, too. People still lose their way on Mount Hood and face death at the hand of unexpected storms. A pioneering spirit of restlessness and adventurousness remains in evidence whenever climbers tackle the seemingly impossible routes. Timeless is the experience of coming to a clearing in the forest, or rounding a bend in the loop highway, and suddenly confronting that magnificent scene: "the mountain" up close, revealed from base to summit. Never before, wrote Palmer of that moment, had he seen "a sight so nobly grand."

It remains so to this day.

John Palmer Spencer

A SIGHT SO NOBLY GRAND

Mount Hood from the south, showing the Timberline Lodge area On 11 October, having followed an Indian trail up one of the ridges of White River Canyon (far right), Palmer crossed this southern face of the mountain, passing the present site of Timberline Lodge and eventually camping near Paradise Park (not pictured). His climb the next day took him around Mississippi Head (a portion of which is visible to the upper left) and up Zigzag Glacier, to a point thought to be somewhere below Crater Rock (which can be seen protruding, at about 10,000 feet, directly below the summit ridge). Rising on the horizon, in southern Washington, is 12,000-foot Mount Adams.

(Al Monner photo. OrHi 86857)

INTO THE MOUNTAINS

Here was the end of the road,
as no wagons had ever gone below this place.

September 29, 1845. This day we traveled about five miles, which brought us to the *Dalles*, or Methodist Missions. Here was the end of our road, as no wagons had ever gone below this place.[1] We found some sixty families in waiting for a passage down the river; and as there were but two small boats running to the Cascade falls, our prospect for a speedy passage was not overly flattering.[2]

September 30. This day we intended to make arrangements for our passage down the river, but we found upon inquiry, that the two boats spoken of were engaged for at least ten days, and that their charges were exorbitant, and would probably absorb what little we had left to pay our way to *Oregon City.* We then determined to make a trip over the mountains, and made inquiries respecting its practicability of some Indians, but could learn nothing definite, excepting that grass, timber and water would be found in abundance; we finally ascertained that a Mr. Barlow and Mr. H. M. Knighton had, with the

---

1. This was the third year of heavy migration to Oregon. Though a train of 112 emigrants had made the journey in 1842, the much larger Great Migration of the following year—roughly 900 emigrants—is most commonly cited as the inauguration of the Oregon Trail. In 1845, Palmer was one of about 3,000 emigrants—twice the number of white settlers already in Oregon.
2. The Cascades rapids (see photograph on pp. x - xi).

The Dalles of the Columbia River

Until 1845, the overland portion of the Oregon Trail ended roughly fifteen miles down river from here, at The Dalles Methodist mission. From there, emigrants bound for the Willamette Valley had no choice but to hire boats or rafts for a risky passage down the Columbia River.

Upon his arrival at The Dalles on 30 September 1845, Joel Palmer found sixty families waiting for two small boats.

The Columbia was at that time a turbulent river, and perhaps nowhere was it more turbulent than at The Dalles. Beginning at legendary Celilo Falls on the eastern end, and culminating fifteen miles down river near the Methodist mission, the river

surged through narrow channels cut in flat, basaltic rock. (Those basalt formations gave rise to the name *dalles*, a French word meaning "flagstones"). Perhaps most striking were the Long Narrows, where for several miles the river "turned on its side" in a

slot less than one hundred yards wide. The Long Narrows and Celilo Falls, both an-
cient Indian fishing grounds, were flooded by construction of The Dalles Dam in 1957.
(Carlton E. Watkins photo.   OrHi 21646)

same object, penetrated some twenty or twenty-five miles into the interior, and found it impracticable. Knighton had returned, but Barlow was yet in the mountains, endeavoring to force a passage; they had been absent six days, with seven wagons in their train, intending to go as far as they could, and if found to be impracticable, to return and go down the river.

We succeeded in persuading fifteen families to accompany us in our trip over the mountains, and immediately made preparations for our march. On the afternoon of the first of October, our preparations were announced as complete, and we took up our line of march; others in the mean time had joined us, and should we fall in with Barlow, our train would consist of some thirty wagons.[3]

But before proceeding with a description of this route, I will enter into a detail of the difficulties undergone by the company of two hundred wagons, which had separated from us at Malheur creek, under the pilotage of Mr. Meek.[4]

It will be remembered that S. L. Meek had induced about two hundred families, with their wagons and stock, to turn off at Malheur, with the view of saving thereby some one hundred and fifty miles travel; and they had started about the last of August. They followed up Malheur creek, keeping up the southern branch, and pursuing a southern course. For a long time they found a very good road, plenty of grass, fuel and water; they left these waters, and directed their course over a rough mountainous country, almost entirely bereft of vegetation, were for many days destitute of water, and when they were so fortunate as to procure this indispensable element, it was found stagnant in pools, unfit even for the use of cattle; but necessity compelled them to the use

----

3. Much later, in an 1878 interview with historian Hubert Howe Bancroft, Palmer claimed that the missionary Marcus Whitman had convinced him of the feasibility of a mountain passage even prior to his arrival at The Dalles on 29 September. It is unclear why Palmer does not mention that alleged encounter here.

4. Before recounting his own efforts in pioneering a wagon route to the Willamette Valley, Palmer digresses to to tell of Stephen Meek's far less fortunate attempt to accomplish a similar feat. Writing in 1846, with knowledge of the difficulty and danger his own party faced, Palmer must have intended a comparison, though his meaning is unclear. Certainly the Meek disaster provides a sobering context for the narrative that follows. Palmer speculates that Meek might have established an important new route to the valley had his followers not pressured him to depart from his original course.

of it. The result was, that it made many of them sick; many of the cattle died, and the majority were unfit for labor. A disease termed camp-fever, broke out among the different companies, of which many became the victims.

They at length arrived at a marshy lake, which they attempted to cross, but found it impracticable; and as the marsh appeared to bear south, and many of them were nearly out of provisions, they came to a determination to pursue a northern course, and strike the Columbia. Meek, however, wished to go south of the lake, but they would not follow him. They turned north, and after a few days' travel arrived at Deshutes or Falls river. They traveled up and down this river, endeavoring to find a passage, but as it ran through rocky *kanyons*, it was impossible to cross.

Their sufferings were daily increasing, their stock of provisions was rapidly wasting away, their cattle were becoming exhausted, and many attached to the company were laboring under severe attacks of sickness;—at length Meek informed them that they were not more than two days' ride from the Dalles. Ten men started on horseback for the Methodist stations, with the view of procuring provisions; they took with them a scanty supply of provisions, intended for the two days' journey. After riding faithfully for ten days, they at last arrived at the Dalles. On their way they encountered an Indian, who furnished them with a fish and a rabbit; this with the provision they had started with, was their only food for the ten days' travel. Upon their arrival at the Dalles they were so exhausted in strength, and the rigidity of their limbs, from riding, was so great, as to render them unable to dismount without assistance. They reached the Dalles the day previous to our arrival.

At this place they met an old mountaineer, usually called Black Harris, who volunteered his services as a pilot. He in company with several others, started in search of the lost company, whom they found reduced to great extremities; their provisions nearly exhausted, and the company weakened by exertion, and despairing of ever reaching the settlements. They succeeded in finding a place where their cattle could be driven down to the river, and made to swim across; after crossing, the bluff had to be ascended. Great difficulty arose in the attempt to effect a passage with the wagons. The means finally resorted to for the transportation of the families and wagons were novel in the extreme. A large rope was swung across the stream and attached to the rocks on either side; a light wagon bed was suspended from this rope with pulleys, to which ropes were attached; this bed served to convey the families and loading in safety across; the wagons were then drawn over the bed of the river by ropes. The passage of this river occupied some two weeks. The distance

*Mount Hood from the east
(near present Dufur),
en route to Tygh Valley*
Heading south from
The Dalles to Tygh Valley,
Palmer and his companions
saw Mount Hood from the
rolling hills east of the
mountain in present Wasco
County. This first portion
of the journey presented
little difficulty; the country
was open and the route had
long served as a thorough-
fare for Indians traveling to
and from The Dalles for
trading and fishing.
(OrHi 84576)

was thirty-five miles to the Dalles, at which place they arrived about the 13th, or 14th of October. Some twenty of their number had perished by disease, previous to their arrival at the Dalles, and a like number were lost, after their arrival, from the same cause. This company has been known by the name of the St. Joseph company; but there were persons from every state of the Union within its ranks. Illinois and Missouri, however, had the largest representation.

The statements I have given are as correct as I could arrive at, from consultation with many of the members. This expedition was unfortunate in the extreme. Although commenced under favorable auspices, its termination assumed a gloomy character.

It has been stated that some members of the Hudson's Bay Company were instrumental in this expedition, but such is not the fact. Whilst I was at Fort Hall, I conversed with Captain Grant respecting the practicability of this same route, and was advised of the fact, that the teams would be unable to get through. The individual in charge at Fort Bois also advised me to the same purport. The censure rests, in the origin of the expedition, upon Meek; but I have not the least doubt but he supposed they could get through in safety. I have understood that a few of the members controlled Meek, and caused him to depart from his original plan. It was his design to have conducted the party to the *Willamette Valley,* instead of going to the Dalles; and the direction he first traveled induced this belief. Meek is yet of the opinion that had he gone round the marshy lake to the south, he would have struck the settlement on the Willamette, within the time required to travel to the Dalles. Had he discovered this route, it would have proved a great saving in the distance. I do not question but that there may be a route found to the south of this, opening into the valley of the Willamette.[5] But I must return again to the subject of my travels.

October 1. At four o'clock, P.M., every thing was ready for our departure, and we pursued our way over the ridge, in a southern course. The country was very rolling, and principally prairie. We found excellent grazing. Our camp was pitched on a small spring branch.

October 2. This day we made about ten miles, crossing several ravines, many of which had running water in them; the country, like that of yesterday's

5. In fact, there had been an Indian trail that crossed the Cascades and followed the North Santiam River into the Willamette Valley. The route, however, was not discovered by whites until 1873.

travel, proved to be very rolling; our camp was situated on a small spring branch, having its source in the mountain.

October 3. This morning I started on horseback in advance of the company, accompanied by one of its members. Our course led us south over a rolling, grassy plain; portions of the road were very stony. After a travel of fourteen miles, we arrived at a long and steep declivity, which we descended, and after crossing the creek at its base, ascended a bluff; in the bottom are seen several small enclosures, where the Indians have cultivated the soil; a few Indian huts may be seen along this stream.[6]

Meek's company crossed Deshute's river near the mouth of this stream, which is five miles distant. After ascending, we turned to the right, directing our course over a level grassy plain for some five miles or more, when we crossed a running branch; five miles brought us to Stony Branch, and to scattering yellow pine timber. Here we found Barlow's company of seven wagons. Barlow was absent at the time, having with three others started into the mountain two days before. We remained with them all night.

October 4. This morning myself and companion, with a scanty supply of provisions for a two days' journey, started on a westerly course into the mountains. From the open ground we could see Mount Hood.[7] Our object was to go south and near to this peak. For five miles the country was alternately prairie and yellow pine; we then ascended a ridge, which ascended gradually to the west. This we followed for ten miles. After the crossing of a little brushy bottom, we took over another ridge for four or five miles, very heavily timbered and densely covered with undergrowth. We descended the ridge for a short distance, and traveled a level bench for four miles; this is covered with very large and tall fir timber; we then descended the mountain, traveling

---

6. These were the Tygh Indians of steep-walled Tygh Valley. Having entered and climbed out of the valley on horseback, Palmer does not mention the difficulty faced by wagons in doing so; according to Lenore Woodcock Walters in *Barlow Road*, six to eight teams were needed to pull one wagon to the top.

7. With the exception of an unsuccessful attempt by Hall J. Kelley to rename it Mount Adams, the mountain had been known to white settlers and explorers as Mount Hood since 1792. In that year, Lieutenant William Broughton of the British Royal Navy, sailing under the command of Captain George Vancouver, sighted the peak from the Columbia River and named it for Lord Samuel Hood, who had signed the original instructions for Vancouver's voyage. Indians, of course, had long known the mountain by other names; "Wy'east" (or "Wa-ye-ast") is the most commonly cited of these, though its origin is unclear.

westward for one and a half miles; we then came to a small branch, which we named Rock creek. After crossing the creek, we ascended a hill for one fourth of a mile, then bore to the left around the hill, through a dense forest of spruce pine. After five miles travel from Rock creek we came to a marshy cedar swamp; we turned to the left, and there found a suitable place for crossing. Here is a stream of from five to six yards in width, when confined to one channel; but in many places it runs over a bottom of two rods in width, strewed with old moss covered logs and roots. The water was extremely clear and cold. Four miles brought us to the top of the bluff of a deep gulf; we turned our course northward for two miles, when darkness overtook us, forcing us to encamp. A little grass was discernible on the mountain sides, which afforded our jaded horses a scanty supply.

October 5. At an early hour this morning, I proceeded down the mountain to the stream at its base. I found the descent very abrupt and difficult; the distance was one half mile. The water was running very rapid; it had the same appearance as the water of the *Missouri*, being filled with white sand. I followed this stream up for some distance, and ascertained that its source was in Mount Hood; and from the appearance of the banks, it seems that its waters swell during the night, overflowing its banks, and subside again by day; it empties into Deshute's river, having a sandy bottom of from two rods to half a mile wide, covered with scrubby pines, and sometimes a slough of alder bushes, with a little grass and rushes.[8] We then ascended the mountain, and as our stock of provisions was barely sufficient to last us through the day, it was found necessary to return to camp. We retraced our steps to where we had struck the bluff, and followed down a short distance where we found the mountain of sufficiently gradual descent to admit the passage of teams; we could then follow up the bottom towards *Mount Hood*, and as we supposed that this peak was the dividing ridge, we had reasonable grounds to hope that we could get through. We then took our trail in the direction of the camp; and late in the evening, tired and hungry, we arrived at Rock creek, where we found our

---

8. The stream is the White River, whose source is the meltwater from White River Glacier on Mount Hood. The qualities noticed by Palmer—high silt content and a daily ebb and flow in volume—are typical of glacial streams. The "mountain" to which Palmer refers is Little Laurel Hill, so called because its thick mountain laurel and extreme steepness were exceeded only by those of the infamous Laurel Hill itself, just west of present Government Camp.

company encamped. Barlow had not yet returned, but we resolved to push forward.

October 6. We remained in camp. As the grazing was poor in the timber, and our loose cattle much trouble to us, we determined to send a party with them to the settlement. The Indians had informed us that there was a trail to the north, which ran over Mount Hood, and thence to Oregon city. This party was to proceed up one of the ridges until they struck this trail, and then follow it to the settlement. Two families decided upon going with this party, and as I expected to have no further use for my horse, I sent him with them. They were to procure provisions and assistance, and meet us on the way. We had forwarded, by a company of cattle-drivers from the Dalles, which started for the settlement on the first of the month, a request that they would send us provisions and assistance; but as we knew nothing of their whereabouts, we had little hope of being benefited by them. The day was spent in making the necessary arrangements for the cattle-drivers, and for working the road. In the afternoon, Barlow and his party returned. They had taken nearly the same route that we had; they had followed up the bluff of this branch of the De Shutes, to within twelve or fifteen miles of Mount Hood, where they supposed they had seen Willamette valley. They had then taken the Indian trail spoken of, and followed it to one of the ridges leading down to the river De Shutes; this they followed, and came out near our camp. We now jointly adopted measures for the prosecution of the work before us.

October 7. Early in the morning, the party designated to drive our loose cattle made their arrangements, and left us. And as we supposed our stock of provisions was insufficient to supply us until these men returned, we dispatched a few men to the Dalles for a beef and some wheat; after which, we divided our company so as that a portion were to remain and take charge of the camp. A sufficient number were to pack provisions, and the remainder were to be engaged in opening the road. All being ready, each one entered upon the duty assigned him with an alacrity and willingness that showed a full determination to prosecute it to completion, if possible. On the evening of the 10th, we had opened a road to the top of the mountain, which we were to descend to the branch of the De Shutes. The side of the mountain was covered with a species of laurel bush, and so thick, that it was almost impossible to pass through it, and as it was very dry we set it on fire. We passed down and encamped on the creek, and during the night the fire had nearly cleared the road on the side of the mountain.

I judged the ravine to be three thousand feet deep. The manner of

A HISTORIC ASCENT

The opinion heretofore entertained,
that this peak could not be ascended to its summit,
I found to be erroneous.

On the morning of October 11th, a consultation was had, when it was determined that Mr. Barlow, Mr. Lock, and myself, should go in advance, and ascertain whether we could find a passage over the main dividing ridge. In the mean time, the remainder of the party were to open the road up the creek bottom as far as they could, or until our return. We took some provision in our pockets, an axe, and one rifle, and started. We followed up this branch about fifteen miles, when we reached a creek, coming in from the left.[1] We followed up this for a short distance, and then struck across to the main fork; and in doing so, we came into a cedar swamp, so covered with heavy timber and brush that it was almost impossible to get through it. We were at least one hour in traveling half a mile. We struck the opening along the other fork, traveled up this about eight miles, and struck the Indian trail spoken of before, near where it comes down the mountain. The last eight miles of our course had been nearly north—a high mountain putting down between the branch and main fork.[2] Where we struck the trail, it turned west into a wide, sandy and stony

---

1. Barlow Creek, hereafter called "the small branch," or simply "the branch," of White River, which Palmer refers to as the "main fork" or "Shutes' fork."
2. Barlow Butte (5069 feet), located less than one mile south of State Highway 35 on the southeast side of Mount Hood.

plain, of several miles in width, extending up to Mount Hood, about seven or eight miles distant, and in plain view.

I had never before looked upon a sight so nobly grand. We had previously seen only the top of it, but now we had a view of the whole mountain. No pen can give an adequate description of this scene. The bottom which we were ascending, had a rise of about three feet to the rod. A perfect mass of rock and gravel had been washed down from the mountain. In one part of the bottom was standing a grove of dead trees, the top of which could be seen; from appearance, the surface had been filled up seventy-five or eighty feet about them. The water came tumbling down, through a little channel, in torrents. Near the upper end of the bottom, the mountains upon either side narrowed in until they left a deep chasm or gulf, where it emerged from the rocky cliffs above. Stretching away to the south, was a range of mountain, which from the bottom appeared to be connected with the mountain on our left. It appeared to be covered with timber far up; then a space of over two miles covered with grass; then a space of more than a mile destitute of vegetation; then commenced the snow, and continued rising until the eye was pained in looking to the top. To our right was a high range, which connected with Mount Hood, covered with timber. The timber near the snow was dead.

We followed this trail for five or six miles, when it wound up a grassy ridge to the left—followed it up to where it connected with the main ridge; this we followed up for a mile, when the grass disappeared, and we came to a ridge entirely destitute of vegetation. It appeared to be sand and gravel, or rather, decomposed material from sandstone crumbled to pieces. Before reaching this barren ridge, we met a party of those who had started with the loose cattle, hunting for some which had strayed off. They informed us that they had lost about one-third of their cattle, and were then encamped on the west side of Mount Hood. We determined to lodge with them, and took the trail over the mountain. In the mean time, the cattle-drovers had found a few head, and traveled with us to their camp.

Soon after ascending and winding round this barren ridge, we crossed a ravine, one or two rods in width, upon the snow, which terminated a short distance below the trail, and extended up to the top of Mount Hood. We then went around the mountain for about two miles, crossing several strips of snow, until we came to a deep kanyon or gulf, cut out by the wash from the mountain above us. A precipitate cliff of rocks, at the head, prevented a passage around it. The hills were of the same material as that we had been traveling over, and were very steep.

*Mount Hood from the
White River*
Following the White River
out of the forest and onto
this "sandy and stony
plain," Palmer gained his
first view, similar to this
one, of the mountain from
base to summit—"a sight so
nobly grand."
(OrHi 89275)

descending is to turn directly to the right, go zigzag for about one hundred yards, then turn short round, and go zigzag until you come under the place where you started from; then to the right, and so on, until you reach the base. In the bottom is a rapid stream, filled with sand. After crossing, we ascended in the same manner, went round the point of a ridge, where we struck another ravine; the sides of this were covered with grass and whortleberry bushes. In this ravine we found the camp of our friends. We reached them about dark; the wind blew a gale, and it was quite cold.[3]

October 12. After taking some refreshment, we ascended the mountain, intending to head the deep ravine, in order to ascertain whether there was any gap in the mountain south of us, which would admit of a pass. From this peak, we overlooked the whole of the mountains. We followed up the grassy ridge for one mile and a half, when it became barren. My two friends began to lag behind, and show signs of fatigue; they finally stopped, and contended that we could not get round the head of the ravine, and that it was useless to attempt an ascent. But I was of a different opinion, and wished to go on. They consented, and followed for half a mile, when they sat down, and requested me to go up to the ledge, and, if we could effect a passage up and get round it, to give them a signal. I did so, and found that by climbing up a cliff of snow and ice, for about forty feet, but not so steep but that by getting upon one cliff, and cutting holes to stand in and hold on by, it could be ascended.[4] I gave the signal, and they came up. In the mean time, I had cut and carved my way up the cliff, and when up to the top was forced to admit that it was something of an undertaking; but as I had arrived safely at the top of the cliff, I doubted not but they could accomplish the same task, and as my moccasins were worn out, and the soles of my feet exposed to the snow, I was disposed to be traveling, and so left them to get up the best way they could. After proceeding about one mile upon the snow, continually winding up, I began to despair of seeing my companions. I came to where a few detached pieces of rock had fallen from the ledge above and rolled down upon the ice and snow, (for the whole mass is

---

3. Palmer was following an Indian route that is now part of the U.S. Forest Service's thirty-five mile Timberline loop trail around Mount Hood. The deep ravine is Zigzag Canyon, and the "cliff of rocks" at the top of the ravine is two-hundred foot high Mississippi Head. The campsite was in the vicinity of Paradise Park, roughly five miles west of the present site of Timberline Lodge.

4. In *Mount Hood: A Complete History,* Jack Grauer suggests that this ice cliff was the terminal wall of Zigzag glacier, which was much larger in 1845.

more like ice than snow); I clambered upon one of these, and waited half an hour.[5] I then rolled stones down the mountain for half an hour; but as I could see nothing of my two friends, I began to suspect that they had gone back, and crossed in the trail. I then went round to the south-east side, continually ascending, and taking an observation of the country south, and was fully of the opinion that we could find a passage through.[6]

The waters of this deep ravine, and of numerous ravines to the north-west, as well as the south-west, form the heads of Big Sandy and Quicksand rivers, which empty into the Columbia, about twenty-five or thirty miles below the Cascade Falls.[7] I could see down this stream some twelve or fifteen miles, where the view was obstructed by a high range coming round from the north-west side, connecting by a low gap with some of the spurs from this peak.[8] All these streams were running through such deep chasms, that it was

---

5. This "ledge," according to Grauer, is probably Illumination Rock.

6. In the original journal, Palmer notes: "The opinion heretofore entertained, that this peak could not be ascended to its summit, I found to be erroneous. I, however, did not arrive at the highest peak, but went sufficiently near to prove its practicability. I judge the diameter of this peak, at the point where the snow remains year round, to be about three miles. At the head of many of the ravines, are perpendicular cliffs of rocks, apparently several thousand feet high; and in some places those cliffs rise so precipitately to the summit, that a passage around is impracticable. I think the southern side affords the easiest ascent. The dark strips observable from a distance, are occasioned by blackish rock, so precipitous as not to admit of the snow lying upon it. The upper strata are of gray sandstone, and seem to be of original formation. There is no doubt, but any of the snow peaks upon this range can be ascended to the summit."

Palmer's description is remarkable not only for its influential assertion that a summit climb was feasible, but also for its accurate sense of scale. Given his complete lack of experience with major mountains, his roughly correct assessment of the diameter of the peak is noteworthy indeed—especially when compared with the belief, espoused in *Mitchell's School Atlas* and other publications, that Mount Hood towered over 18,000 feet high. Palmer's observation of "gray sandstone" is false, and indicates that he did not understand the volcanic origin of the mountain.

7. This should read Big Sandy or Quicksand River; both were names for the Sandy. Palmer observes correctly that all of the meltwater from Mount Hood's western slopes, including the Zigzag river below him, eventually drains into the Sandy.

8. This is Zigzag Mountain, the long ridge on the west side of Mount Hood that separates the Sandy and Zigzag River valleys. Its highest point, near Burnt Lake, is 4971 feet.

impossible to pass them with teams. To the south, were two ranges of mountains, connecting by a low gap with this peak, and winding round until they terminated near Big Sandy.[9] I observed that a stream, heading near the base of this peak and running south-east for several miles, there appeared to turn to the west. This I judged to be the head waters of Clackamis, which empties into the Willamette, near Oregon city; but the view was hid by a high range of mountains putting down in that direction.[10] A low gap seemed to connect this stream, or some other, heading in this high range, with the low bottoms immediately under the base of this peak. I was of the opinion that a pass might be found between this peak and the first range of mountains, by digging down some of the gravel hills;[11] and if not, there would be a chance of passing between the first and second ranges, through this gap to the branch of Clackamis; or, by taking some of the ranges of mountains and following them down, could reach the open ground near the Willamette, as there appeared to be spurs extending in that direction. I could also see a low gap in the direction from where we crossed the small branch, coming up the creek on the 11th, towards several small prairies south of us.[12] It appeared, that if we could get a road opened to that place, our cattle could range about these prairies until we could find a passage for the remainder of the way.

The day was getting far advanced, and we had no provisions, save each of us a small biscuit; and knowing that we had at least twenty-five miles to travel, before reaching those working on the road, I hastened down the mountain. I had no difficulty in finding a passage down; but I saw some deep

---

9. The nearest of these two long ridges is Tom Dick and Harry Mountain, which rises above Mirror Lake and now forms part of the Ski Bowl ski resort; behind it lies Hunchback Mountain.

10. In fact, this is not the head of the Clackamas River, which is in a drainage area south of Palmer's location; it is almost certainly the Salmon River, which winds around Hunchback Mountain and eventually flows into the Sandy.

11. This route passed through what is now Government Camp and down rocky Laurel Hill, and would become the eventual route of Barlow Road and roughly today's U.S. Highway 26.

12. This crucial "low gap" is Barlow Pass (4155 feet), summit of the eventual Barlow Road. It is commemorated today with a marker next to State Highway 35, four miles east of Government Camp.

ravines and crevices in the ice which alarmed me, as I was compelled to travel over them. The snow and ice had melted underneath, and in many places had left but a thin shell upon the surface; some of them had fallen in and presented hideous looking caverns.[13] I was soon out of danger, and upon the east side of the deep ravine I saw my two friends slowly winding their way up the mountain. They had gone to the foot of the ledge, and as they wore boots, and were much fatigued, they abandoned the trip, and returned down the mountain to the trail, where I joined them. We there rested awhile, and struck our course for one of the prairies which we had seen from the mountain. On our way we came to a beautiful spring of water, surrounded with fine timber; the ground was covered with whortle berry bushes, and many of them hanging full of fruit, we halted, ate our biscuit, gathered berries, and then proceeded down the mountain.

After traveling about ten miles, we reached the prairie. It was covered with grass, and was very wet. A red sediment of about two inches in depth covered the surface of the ground in the grass, such as is found around mineral springs. A beautiful clear stream of water was running through the prairie, in a south-east direction. We had seen a prairie about two miles further south, much larger than this, which we supposed to be dry.[14] We now took our course for camp, intending to strike through the gap to the mouth of the small branch; but we failed in finding the right *shute*, and came out into the bottom, three miles above where we had first struck the cattle or Indian trail. We then took down the bottom, and arrived in camp about eleven o'clock at night; and although not often tired, I was willing to acknowledge that I was near being so. I certainly was hungry, but my condition was so much better than that of my two friends, that I could not murmur. Our party had worked the road up to the small branch, where they were encamped.

---

13. Such crevasses are no longer encountered on Zigzag Glacier. Their presence in 1845, according to Grauer, indicates that the glacier has shrunk considerably since that time.

14. Grauer claims that the "wet prairie" is Summit Meadows on Still Creek; by extension, the larger, drier clearing would be Red Top Meadow slightly to the southeast. It is also possible that Palmer's wet prairie is the marshy meadow at Government Camp, and that Summit Meadows, two miles further south, is the "dry" one.

STORM CLOUDS

I began for the first time to falter,
and was at a stand to know what course to pursue.

On the morning of the 13th of October we held a consultation, and determined upon the future movements of the company. The party designated to bring us provisions had performed that service; but the amount of our provisions was nearly exhausted, and many of the party had no means of procuring more. Some of them began to despair of getting through this season. Those left with the camp were unable to keep the cattle together, and a number of them had been lost. The Indians had stolen several horses, and a variety of mishaps occurred, such as would necessarily follow from a company so long remaining in one position. They were now on a small creek, five miles from Stony hill, which we called Camp creek, and near the timber.[1] It was impossible to keep more than one third of the men working at the road; the remainder were needed to attend the camp and pack provisions. It was determined to send a party and view out the road, through to the open country, near the mouth of Clackamis, whilst the others were to open the road as far as the big prairie; a number sufficient to bring up the teams and loose cattle, (for a number of families with their cattle had joined since ours left, and portions

---

1. Camp creek was the wagon train's main camp near the White River, and should not be confused with the previously mentioned encampment of the road clearing party. It is at the latter of the two, further west on Barlow Creek, that Palmer and the other leaders hold their "consultation."

of our company did not send their loose cattle) to a grassy prairie in this bottom, and near the mouth of this creek, as the time required to pack provisions to those working on the road would be saved. All being arranged, the next thing was to designate the persons to go ahead of the party, and if found practicable to return with provisions and help; or at all events to ascertain whether the route were practicable.

It was determined that I should undertake this trip. I asked only one man to accompany me. We took our blankets, a limited supply of provisions, and one light axe, and at eight o'clock in the morning set out. I was satisfied that the creek which we were then on, headed in the low gap seen from Mount Hood; and the party were to open the road up this branch. But as I was to precede them, I passed up this creek for about eight or ten miles, when I discovered the low gap, went through it, and at noon arrived at the wet prairie, which we had visited the day before. The route was practicable, but would require great labor to remove the timber, and cut out the underbrush.

We halted at the creek and took some refreshment; we then struck for the low gap between the first range of mountains running west, and the base of Mount Hood, and traveled through swamps, small prairies, brush, and heavy timber for about twelve miles, when we found the labor necessary to open a wagon road in this direction, to be greater than we could possibly bestow upon it before the rainy season. We determined to try some other route, retraced our steps six or seven miles, and then bore to the right around the base of the mountain, when we struck into an old Indian trail. This we followed for seven or eight miles, through the gap I had seen from Mount Hood.[2] It is a rolling bottom of about four or five miles in width, and extending from the base of Mount Hood south for ten or twelve miles. The trail wound around the mountain, but as its course was about that we wished to travel, we followed it until it ran out at the top of the mountain. We then took the ridge west, and traveled until dark; but as the moon shone bright, and the timber was not very thick, we turned an angle down the mountain to the left, to procure water. We traveled about three miles, and struck upon a small running branch; this we followed, until owing to the darkness, we were compelled to encamp, much fatigued, and somewhat disheartened.

---

2. Having tried and rejected the gap on the Government Camp side of Tom Dick and Harry Mountain, Palmer and his companion were now pushing around the back of the ridge through Still Creek valley.

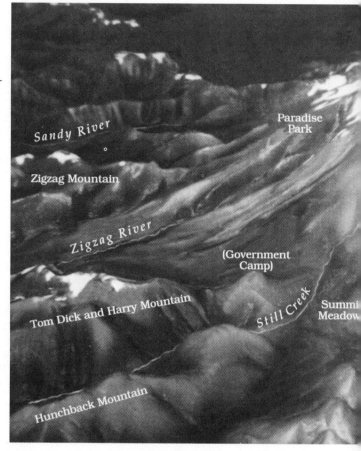

Aerial view of Mount Hood, showing Timberline Lodge
Joel Palmer explored much of this terrain in his scouting mission of 11 to 15 October 1845.

On the eleventh, Palmer, Sam Barlow, and a man named Lock left their camp at the confluence of the White River and Barlow Creek, followed the White River approximately to Mount Hood's timberline, and traveled six miles west to a camp near Paradise Park. In so doing, they passed the present site of Timberline Lodge and traversed Zigzag Canyon. The next day, Palmer ascended, in an eastward direction, Zigzag Glacier, to a point somewhere below Crater Rock (pictured just below the summit ridge in the center). After descending and rejoining his two companions, who had tired and stayed behind, Palmer made a long trek, via Summit Meadows, back to the White River camp. He and an unidentified man spent the following two days exploring possible passes he had spotted from high on Mount Hood. They followed Barlow Creek up to Barlow Pass—the "low gap"— and continued west, through Summit Meadows and

present Government Camp, to survey both possible routes around Tom Dick and Harry Mountain. That route was developed into Barlow Road the following summer and, eventually, into a portion of the Mount Hood Loop Highway—U.S. Highway 26 and State Highway 35.

This view of the mountain was created using a computer program to alter a photograph of the relief model on display in Timberline's Wy'east day lodge. The model was produced by the U.S. Forest Service from topographic maps.

October 14. At daylight we were on the way. My moccasins, which the night before had received a pair of soles, in yesterday's tramp had given way, and in traveling after night my feet had been badly snagged, so that I was in poor plight for walking; but as there was no alternative, we started down the mountain, and after traveling a few miles I felt quite well and was able to take the lead. We traveled about three miles, when we struck a large creek which had a very rapid current, over a stony bottom.[3] I had hoped to find a bottom of sufficient width to admit of a wagon road, but after following down this stream six miles, I was satisfied that it would not do to attempt it this season.

The weather, which had been entirely clear for months, had through the night began to cloud up; and in the morning the birds, squirrels, and every thing around, seemed to indicate the approach of a storm. I began for the first time to falter, and was at a stand to know what course to pursue. I had understood that the rainy season commenced in October, and that the streams rose to an alarming height, and I was sensible that if we crossed the branch of the Deshutes, which headed in Mount Hood, and the rainy season set in, we could not get back, and to get forward would be equally impossible; so that in either event starvation would be the result. And as I had been very active in inducing others to embark in the enterprise, my conscience would not allow me to go on and thus endanger so many families. But to go back, and state to them the difficulties to be encountered, and the necessity of taking some other course, seemed to be my duty. I therefore resolved to return, and recommend selecting some suitable place for a permanent camp, build a cabin, put in such effects as we could not pack out, and leave our wagons and effects in the charge of some persons until we could return the next season, unincumbered with our families and cattle, and finish the road;—or otherwise to return to the Dalles with our teams, where we could leave our baggage in charge of the missionaries, and then descend the Columbia. And when my mind was fully made up, we were not long in carrying it into execution.

We accordingly ascended the mountain, as it was better traveling than in the bottom. The distance to the summit was about four miles, and the way was sometimes so steep as to render it necessary to pull up by the bushes. We then traveled east until we reached the eastern point of this mountain, and descended to the bottom, the base of which we had traversed the day before. We

---

3. This is probably Camp Creek (not to be confused with the White River wagon camp of the same name) not far above present Rhododendron.

then struck for the trail, soon found it, and followed it until it led us to the southern end of the wet prairie. We then struck for the lower gap in the direction of the camp, crossed over and descended the branch to near its mouth, where we found four of our company clearing the road, the remainder having returned to Camp creek for teams. But as we had traveled about fifty miles this day, I was unable to reach the camp.

October 15. This morning we all started for camp, carrying with us our tools and provisions. We reached camp about two P.M. Many of our cattle could not be found, but before night nearly all were brought into camp. The whole matter was then laid before the company, when it was agreed that we should remove over to the bottom, near the small creek, and if the weather was unfavorable, leave our baggage and wagons, and pack out the families as soon as possible. But as some were out of provisions, it was important that a messenger should be sent on ahead for provisions, and horses to assist in packing out. Mr. Buffum, and lady, concluded to pack out what articles they could, and leave a man to take charge of the teams and cattle, until he returned with other horses. He kindly furnished me with one of his horses to ride to the settlement. He also supplied the wife of Mr. Thompson with a horse. Mr. Barlow and Mr. Rector made a proposition to continue working the road until the party could go to and return from the valley; they agreeing to insure the safety of the wagons, if compelled to remain through the winter, by being paid a certain per cent upon the valuation. This proposition was thought reasonable by some, and it was partially agreed to. And as there were some who had no horses with which to pack out their families, they started on foot for the valley, designing to look out a road as they passed along. Some men in the mean time were to remain with the camp, which as above stated was to be removed to the small branch on Shutes' fork; and those who intended pushing out at once, could follow up it to the Indian trail. This all being agreed upon, arrangements were made accordingly.

NO LITTLE TOIL AND HARDSHIP

*Our horses were shivering with the cold,
the rain had put out our fire,
and it seemed as though
every thing had combined to render us miserable.*

October 16. The morning was lowering, with every indication of rain. Messrs. Barlow and Rector started on the trip.[1] All hands were making arrangements for moving the camp. In the mean time Mr. Buffum and his lady, and Mrs. Thompson, were ready to start. I joined them, and we again set out for the settlement. We had traveled about two miles when it commenced raining, and continued raining slightly all day. We encamped on the bottom of Shutes' fork, near the small branch. It rained nearly all night.

On the morning of the 17th October after our horses had filled themselves, we packed up and started. It was still raining. We followed up this bottom to the trail, and then pursued the trail over Mount Hood. Whilst going over this mountain the rain poured down in torrents, it was foggy, and very cold. We arrived at the deep ravine at about four P.M., and before we ascended the opposite bank it was dark; but we felt our way over the ridge, and round the point to the grassy run. Here was grazing for our tired horses, and we dismounted. Upon the side of the mountain, where were a few scattering trees, we found some limbs and sticks, with which we succeeded in getting a little

---

1. In an apparent change of plans, the two men hoped to reach Oregon City on foot and bring back additional horses and provisions. Having brought food for an estimated two day trip to the settlement, they endured enormous hardship when the journey actually took six days.

fire. We then found a few sticks and constructed a tent, covering it blankets, which protected our baggage and the two women. Mr. Buffum and myself stood shivering in the rain around the fire, and when daylight appeared, it gave us an opportunity to look at each others' lank visages. Our horses were shivering with the cold, the rain had put out our fire, and it seemed as though every thing had combined to render us miserable. After driving our horses round awhile, they commenced eating; but we had very little to eat, and were not troubled much in cooking it.

October 18. As soon as our horses had satisfied themselves we packed up and ascended the mountain over the ridge, and for two miles winding around up and down over a rough surface covered with grass. The rain was falling in torrents, and it was so foggy that we could barely see the trail. We at length went down a ridge two miles, when we became bewildered in the thick bushes. The trail had entirely disappeared. We could go no farther. The two women sat upon their horses in the rain, whilst I went back to search for the right trail; Buffum endeavoring to make his way down the mountain. I rambled about two miles up the mountain, where I found the right trail, and immediately returned to inform them of it. Buffum had returned, and of course had not found the trail. We then ascended the mountain to the trail, when a breeze sprung up and cleared away the fog. We could then follow the trail.

We soon saw a large band of cattle coming up the mountain, and in a short time met a party of men following them. They had started from the Dalles about eight days before, and encamped that night four or five miles below, and as it was a barren spot, their cattle had strayed to the mountain to get grass. But what was very gratifying, they informed us that a party of men from Oregon city, with provisions for our company had encamped with them, and were then at their camp. We hastened down the mountain, and in a few hours arrived at the camp. But imagine our feelings when we learned that those having provisions for us, had despaired of finding us, and having already been out longer than was expected, had returned to the settlement, carrying with them all the provisions, save what they had distributed to these men. We were wet, cold, and hungry, and would not be likely to overtake them. We prevailed upon one of the men whom we found at the camp, to mount one of our horses, and follow them. He was absent about ten minutes, when he returned and informed us that they were coming. They soon made their appearance. This revived us, and for awhile we forgot that we were wet and cold. They had gone about six miles back, when some good spirit induced them to return to camp, and make one more effort to find us. The camp was half a mile from the creek, and we had nothing but two small coffee-pots, and a few tin cups, to carry water in; but this was trifling, as the rain was still pouring down upon us. We speedily made a good fire, and set to work making a tent, which we soon accomplished, and the two women prepared us a good supper of bread and coffee. It was a rainy night, but we were as comfortable as the circumstances would admit.

October 19. After breakfast, the drovers left us; and as the party which had brought us provisions had been longer out than had been contemplated, Mr. Stewart and Mr. Gilmore wished to return. It was determined that Mr. Buffum, the two females, Mr. Stewart, and Mr. N. Gilmore, should go on to the settlement, and that Mr. C. Gilmore, and the Indian who had been sent along to assist in driving the horses, and myself, should hasten on with the provisions to the camp. We were soon on the way, and climbing up the mountain. The horses were heavily loaded, and in many places the mountain was very slippery, and of course we had great difficulty in getting along. It was still raining heavily, and the fog so thick that a person could not see more than fifteen feet around. We traveled about two miles up the mountain, when we found that whilst it had been raining in the valley it had been snowing on the mountain. The trail was so covered with snow that it was difficult to find it, and, to increase our difficulty, the Indian refused to go any farther. We showed him the whip, which increased his speed a little, but he soon forgot it, was very sulky, and would not assist in driving.[2] We at length arrived at the deep ravine; here there was no snow, and we passed it without serious difficulty. Two of our packs coming off, and rolling down the hill, was the only serious trouble that we had. When we ascended the hill to the eastern side of the gulf, we found the snow much deeper than upon the western side; besides, it had drifted, and rendered the passage over the strip of the old snow somewhat dangerous, as in many places the action of the water had melted the snow upon the under side, and left a thin shell over the surface, and in some places holes had melted through. We were in danger of falling into one of these pits. Coming to one of these ravines where the snow had drifted very much, I dismounted in order to pick a trail through, but before this was completed, our horses started down the bank. I had discovered two of these pits, and ran to head the horses and turn them; but my riding horse started to run, and went directly between the

---

2. As Terence O'Donnell noted in *An Arrow in the Earth* (p. 38), "Use of the lash on Indians as well as whites was common practice and, in many cases, was prescribed by law."

two pits; his weight jarred the crust loose, and it fell in, presenting a chasm of some twenty-five or thirty feet in depth, but the horse, being upon the run, made his way across the pit. The other horses, hearing the noise and seeing the pits before them, turned higher up, where the snow and ice were thicker, and all reached the opposite side in safety.

Our Indian friend now stopped, and endeavored to turn the horses back, but two to one was an uneven game, and it was played to his disadvantage. He wanted an additional blanket; this I promised him, and he consented to go on. We soon met two Indians, on their way from the Dalles to Oregon city; our Indian conversed with them awhile, and then informed us of his intention to return with them. Whilst parleying with him, a party of men from our camp came up the mountain with their cattle; they had driven their teams to the small branch of the De Shutes, twelve miles below the mountain, where they had left the families, and started out with their cattle before the stream should get too high to cross. Whilst we were conversing with these men, our Indian had succeeded in getting one loose horse, and the one which he was riding, so far from the band of pack-horses that, in the fog, we could not see him, and he returned to the settlement with the two Indians we had just met.

Our horses were very troublesome to drive, as they had ate nothing for thirty-six hours; but we succeeded in getting them over the snow, and down to the grassy ridge, where we stopped for the night. My friend Gilmore shouldered a bag of flour, carried it half a mile down the mountain to a running branch, opened the sack, poured in water, and mixed up bread. In the mean time, I had built a fire. We wrapped the dough around sticks and baked it before the fire, heated water in our tin cups and made a good dish of tea, and passed a very comfortable night. It had ceased raining before sunset, and the morning was clear and pleasant; we forgot the past, and looked forward to a bright future.

October 20. At 8 o'clock we packed up, took the trail down the mountain to the gravelly bottom, and then down the creek to the wagon-camp, which we reached at 3 P.M.; and if we had not before forgotten our troubles, we certainly should have done so upon arriving at camp. Several families were entirely out of provisions, others were nearly so, and all were expecting to rely upon their poor famished cattle. True, this would have prevented starvation; but it would have been meagre diet, and there was no certainty of having cattle long, as there was but little grass. A happier set of beings I never saw, and the thanks bestowed upon us by these families would have compensated for no little toil and hardship. They were supplied with an amount of provisions sufficient to last them until they could reach the settlements. After waiting one day, Mr. Gilmore left the camp for the settlement, taking with him three families; others started about the same time, and in a few days all but three families had departed. These were Mr. Barlow's, Mr. Rector's, and Mr. Caplinger's, all of whom had gone on to the settlement for horses. Ten men yet remained at camp, and, after selecting a suitable place for our wagon-yard, we erected a cabin for the use of those who were to remain through the winter, and to stow away such of our effects as we could not pack out. This being done, nothing remained but to await the return of those who had gone for pack horses. We improved the time in hunting and gathering berries, until the 25th, when four of us, loaded with heavy packs, started on foot for the valley of the Willamette.

But before entering upon this trip, I will state by what means the timely assistance afforded us in the way of provisions was effected. The first party starting for the settlement from the Dalles, after we had determined to take the mountain route, carried the news to Oregon city that we were attempting a passage across the Cascade mountains, and that we should need provisions.[3] The good people of that place immediately raised by donation about eleven hundred pounds of flour, over one hundred pounds of sugar, some tea, &c., hired horses, and the Messrs. Gilmore and Mr. Stewart volunteered to bring these articles to us. The only expense we were asked to defray was the hire of the horses. They belonged to an Indian chief, and of course he had to be paid. The hire was about forty dollars, which brought the flour to about four dollars per hundred, as there were about one thousand pounds when they arrived. Those who had the means paid at once, and those who were unable to pay gave their due bills. Many of the families constructed pack saddles and put them on oxen, and, in one instance, a feather bed was rolled up and put upon an ox; but the animal did not seem to like his load, and ran into the woods, scattering the feathers in every direction: he was finally secured, but not until the bed was ruined. In most cases, the oxen performed well.

---

3. It will be recalled that Palmer referred to this party of cattle drivers on 6 October (p. 13), expressing "little hope of being benefited by them."

TO THE VALLEY

We beheld Oregon and the Falls of the Willamette
at the same moment....
we stopped, and in this moment of happiness recounted our toils.

In the afternoon of the 25th October, accompanied by Messrs. Creighton, Farwell, and Buckley, I again started to the valley. We had traveled but a short distance when we met Barlow and Rector, who had been to the settlement. They had some horses, and expected others in a short time. They had induced a few families whom they met near Mount Hood to return with them, and try their chance back to the Dalles; but, after waiting one day, they concluded to try the mountain trip again. We traveled up the bottom to the trail, where we encamped; about this time, it commenced raining, which continued through the night.

October 26. This morning at eight o'clock, we were on the way. It was rainy, and disagreeable traveling. We followed the trail over the main part of the mountain, when we overtook several families, who had left us on the twenty-second. Two of the families had encamped the night before in the bottom of the deep ravine; night overtook them, and they were compelled to camp, without fuel, or grass for cattle or horses. Water they had in plenty, for it was pouring down upon them all the night. One of their horses broke loose, and getting to the provision sack, destroyed the whole contents. There were nine persons in the two families, four of them small children, and it was about eighty miles to the nearest settlement. The children, as well as the grown people, were nearly barefoot, and poorly clad. Their names were Powell and

33

Senters. Another family by the name of Hood, had succeeded in getting up the gravelly hill, and finding grass for their animals, and a little fuel, had shared their scanty supply with these two families, and when we overtook them they were all encamped near each other. We gave them about half of our provisions, and encamped near them. Mr. Hood kindly furnished us with a wagon cover, with which we constructed a tent, under which we rested for the night.

October 27. The two families who had lost their provisions succeeded in finding a heifer that belonged to one of the companies traveling in advance of us. In rambling upon the rocky cliffs above the trail for grass, it had fallen down the ledge, and was so crippled as not to be able to travel. The owners had left it, and as the animal was in good condition, it was slaughtered and the meat cured.

After traveling four miles through the fresh snow, (which had fallen about four inches deep during the night) we came to where the trail turned down to the Sandy. We were glad to get out of the snow, as we wore moccasins, and the bottoms being worn off, our feet were exposed. Two miles brought us to where we left the Sandy, and near the place where we met the party with provisions; here we met Mr. Buffum, Mr. Lock, and a Mr. Smith, with fourteen pack-horses, going for effects to Fort Deposit—the name which we had given our wagon camp.

The numerous herds of cattle which had passed along had so ate up the grass and bushes, that it was with great difficulty the horses could procure a sufficiency to sustain life. Among the rest, was a horse for me; and as I had a few articles at the fort, Mr. Buffum was to take the horse along and pack them out. Two of his horses were so starved as to be unable to climb the mountains, and we took them back with us. The weather by this time had cleared up; we separated, and each party took its way.

A short distance below this, our trail united with one which starting from the Dalles, runs north of Mount Hood, and until this season was the only trail traveled by the whites.[1] We proceeded down the Sandy, crossing it several times, through thickets of spruce and alder, until we arrived at the forks, which

---

1. This route was the precursor of scenic Lolo Pass Road on the north side of Mount Hood. It was pioneered by Methodist missionary Daniel Lee in 1838 as a cattle trail linking the Willamette mission near present Salem with the mission at The Dalles. Barlow and Palmer could have attempted to travel this route with their wagons, but apparently they had heard at The Dalles that it was a less desirable route.

were about fifteen miles from the base of Mount Hood.[2] The bottom of the Sandy is similar to the branch of De Shutes which we ascended; but in most cases the gravel and stones are covered with moss; portions of it are entirely destitute of vegetation. The mountains are very high, and are mostly covered with timber. At a few points are ledges of grayish rock, but the greater part of the mountain is composed of sand and gravel; it is much cut up by deep ravines, or kanyons. The trail is sometimes very difficult to follow, on account of the brush and logs; about our camp are a few bunches of brakes, which the horses eat greedily. The stream coming in from the south-east is the one which I followed down on the 14th, and from appearance I came within five miles of the forks. The bottom in this vicinity is more than a mile wide, and is covered with spruce, hemlock and alder, with a variety of small bushes.

October 28. We started early, and after having traveled several miles, found a patch of good grass, where we halted our horses for an hour. We then traveled on, crossing the Sandy three times. This is a rapid stream; the water is cold, and the bottom very stony. We made about fifteen or sixteen miles only, as we could not get our horses along faster. We struck into a road recently opened for the passage of wagons. Mr. Taylor, from Ohio, who had left our company with his family and cattle on the 7th, had arrived safely in the valley, and had procured a party of men and had sent them into the mountains to meet us at the crossing of Sandy. They had come up this far, and commenced cutting the road toward the settlements. After traveling this road five or six miles we came upon their camp, where we again found something to eat; our provisions having been all consumed. The road here runs through a flat or bottom of several miles in width, and extending ten or twelve miles down the Sandy; it bears towards the north, whilst the creek forms an elbow to the south. The soil is good, and is covered with a very heavy growth of pine and white cedar timber. I saw some trees of white cedar that were seven feet in diameter, and at least one hundred and fifty feet high. I measured several old trees that had fallen, which were one hundred and eighty feet in length, and about six feet in diameter at the root. We passed some small prairies and several beautiful streams, which meandered through the timber. The ground lies sloping to the south, as it is on the north side of the creek. In the evening it commenced raining a little. We remained at this camp all night.

---

2. Here the Zigzag River flows into the Sandy from the southeast, near the town of Zigzag.

October 29. This morning, after breakfast, we parted with our friends and pursued our way. We soon ascended a ridge which we followed for seven or eight miles, alternately prairie and fern openings. In these openings the timber is not large, but grows rather scrubby. There are numerous groves of beautiful pine timber, tall and straight. The soil is of a reddish cast, and very mellow, and I think would produce well. We came to the termination of this ridge and descended to the bottom, which has been covered with heavy timber, but which has been killed by fire. From this ridge we could see several others, of a similar appearance, descending gradually towards the west.

We here crossed the creek or river, which was deep and rapid; and as our horses were barely able to carry themselves, we were compelled to wade the stream. Buckly had been sick for several days, and not able to carry his pack; and if at other times I regretted the necessity of being compelled to carry his pack, I now found it of some advantage in crossing the stream, as it assisted in keeping me erect. Buckly in attempting to wade across, had so far succeeded as to reach the middle of the stream, where he stopped, and was about giving way when he was relieved by Farwell, a strong athletic yankee from the state of Maine. In crossing a small bottom, one of the horses fell; we were unable to raise him to his feet, and were compelled to leave him. The other we succeeded in getting to the top of the hill, where we were also compelled to leave him. The former died, but the latter was taken in a few days after by those who were opening the road. After being relieved of the burthen of the two horses, we pushed forward on foot, as fast as Buckly's strength and our heavy packs would allow; and as it had been raining all day, our packs were of double their former weight. At dark we met a party of men who had been through with a drove of cattle, and were returning with pack horses for the three families who were yet at Fort Deposit. We encamped with them. After crossing the Sandy our course was south-west, over a rolling and prairie country. The prairie, as well as the timber land, was covered with fern. The soil was of a reddish cast, and very mellow, as are all the ridges leading from the mountain to the Willamette or Columbia river. We traveled this day sixteen or seventeen miles.

October 30. This morning was rainy as usual. Four miles brought us to the valley of the Clackamis, which was here five or six miles wide. The road was over a rolling country similar to that we passed over on yesterday. To the left of the trail we saw a house at the foot of the hill; we made for it, and found some of our friends who had started from camp with C. Gilmore. The claim was held by a man named McSwain. We tarried here until the morning of the 31st, when we again started for Oregon city. Our trail ran for five or six miles along the foot of the hill, through prairie and timber land. The soil looks good, but is rather inclined to gravel; numerous streams flow down from the high ground, which rises gradually to a rolling fern plain, such as we traveled over on the 28th, and 29th. We then continued upon the high ground seven or eight miles, alternately through timber and fern prairies. We then turned down to Clackamis bottom, which is here about one mile wide; this we followed down for three miles, when night overtook us, and we put up at Mr. Hatche's, having spent just one month in the Cascade mountains.

November 1. This morning we left Hatche's and in two miles travel we reached the crossings of the Clackamis river. At this point it is one hundred and fifty yards wide, the banks of gentle descent, the water wending its way for the noble Columbia over a pebbly bottom. Here is a village of about twenty families, inhabited by the Clackamis Indians, who are few in number, apparently harmless, and caring for nothing more than a few fish, a little game, or such subsistence as is barely sufficient to support life. There are but two or three houses in the village; they are made by setting up side and centre posts in the ground, the latter being the highest, to receive a long pole to uphold puncheons split out of cedar, which form the covering; the sides are enclosed with the same material, in an upright position. These puncheons are held to their places by leather thongs, fastened around them to the poles that lay upon the posts. After examining this little community, the remains of a once powerful and warlike people, we obtained the use of their canoes, crossed over the river, and after two miles further travel we reached a point that had long been a desired object; where we were to have rest and refreshment.

We were now at the place destined at no distant period to be an important point in the commercial history of the Union — Oregon City. Passing through the timber that lies to the east of the city, we beheld Oregon and the Falls of the Willamette at the same moment. We were so filled with gratitude that we had reached the settlements of the white man, and with admiration at the appearance of the large sheet of water rolling over the Falls, that we stopped, and in this moment of happiness recounted our toils, in thought, with more rapidity than tongue can express or pen write. Here we hastily scanned over the distance traveled, from point to point, which we computed to be in miles as follows, viz: From Independence to Fort Laramie, 629 miles; from Fort Laramie to Fort Hall, 585 miles; from Fort Hall to Fort Bois, 281 miles; from Fort Bois to the Dalles, 305 miles; from the Dalles to Oregon City, (by the wagon route south of Mount Hood) 160 miles, making the total distance from Independence to Oregon City, 1960 miles. Actual measurement will vary these distances, most

Oregon City—"The settlement"--in 1845

Joel Palmer reached Oregon City on 1 November 1845, "filled with gratitude." It was the very year in which this watercolor was painted by Henry Warre. Palmer had left The Dalles, with its view of the northeast face of Mount Hood, exactly one month before. Now, after tracing a one-hundred-and-thirty mile arc around Mount Hood, he beheld its western side, so familiar to Portlanders today. In that month Joel Palmer had seen how the mountain dominates the skyline from all sides.
(OrHi 791)

probably lessen them; and it is very certain, that by bridging the streams, the travel will be much shortened, by giving to it a more direct course, and upon ground equally favorable for a good road.[3]

---

3. Most of the emigrants had reached Oregon City by this time, but several families, including Barlow's, had delayed at Fort Deposit and would not arrive until 25 December.

FURTHER READING

IN THE LITERATURE on Mount Hood, Fred H. McNeil's Wy'*east*, *'The Mountain'* (originally published in 1937, and reprinted as *McNeil's Mount Hood*, The Zig Zag Papers, 1990), is widely regarded as the classic history, covering Indian legends, geology, the pioneer period, and modern activities on the mountain through the 1930s. McNeil knew and loved his subject—he was an avid mountaineer as well as a journalist—and it shows in his lively and informed book. Also invaluable are Jack Grauer's *Mount Hood: A Complete History* (1975), a richly illustrated and exhaustively detailed guide to the mountain's past; and Don and Roberta Lowe's *Mount Hood: Portrait of a Magnificent Mountain* (The Caxton Printers, Ltd., 1975), a collection of color and archival photographs accompanied by historical essays.

For additional reading on Joel Palmer see Terence O'Donnell's *An Arrow in the Earth: General Joel Palmer and the Indians of Oregon* (Oregon Historical Society Press, 1991), a compelling portrait not only of Palmer's tenure as superintendent of Indian affairs in the Oregon Territory, but of the entire fabric of early Oregon history; and Palmer's own *Journal of Travels Over the Rocky Mountains* (Oregon Historical Society Press, 1993), the classic Oregon Trail travel journal from which *A Sight So Nobly Grand* is excerpted.

Barlow Road (Wasco and Clackamas County Historical Societies, 1991) is an anthology of essays about the journey around Mount Hood in 1845 and the subsequent history of the route as a toll road. Malcolm Clark, Jr.'s *Eden Seekers: The Settlement of Oregon, 1818-1862* (Hougton-Mifflin, 1981) is an engaging and incisive introduction to early Oregon history, including the Oregon Trail.

For a useful history of mountaineering, from its European origins to the first ascent of Mount Everest in 1953, see James Ramsey Ullman's *The Age of Mountaineering* (J.B. Lippincott Company, 1954).

The single most important reference work on the state of Oregon is *Oregon Geographic Names*. This Oregon Historical Society Press book, now in its sixth edition, has been produced by Lewis A. McArthur and his son Lewis L. McArthur.

JOEL PALMER: A CHRONOLOGY

JOEL PALMER IS MOST NOTED for his leadership of wagon trains on the Oregon Trail and his principled service, during an especially bitter period of Indian-white relations in the 1850s, as the Oregon Territory's superintendent of Indian affairs.

Unlike most who emigrated to the Oregon Country in the 1840s, Palmer made the journey a first time without his family, to see whether the place lived up to its extravagant reputation. Evidently it did. In 1847, he returned with his wife and five children to begin a new life. On each of his two trips to Oregon, Palmer established himself as a leader: the first time, by serving as captain of a company of thirty wagons and pioneering, along with Sam Barlow of Kentucky, the route later known as Barlow Road; and the second time, by leading one of the largest emigrations ever—some four to five thousand people in all. His *Journal of Travels Over the Rocky Mountains*, comprised of notes he made on the first trip, was published in 1847 and served as a practical guidebook for several years before eventually becoming a classic historical text.

Only months after arriving to stay, Palmer was appointed commissary general and eventually peace negotiator in the Cayuse Indian War of 1848. He experienced firsthand the explosiveness of Indian-white relations in Oregon.

But no experience could have adequately prepared Palmer for the challenge he faced, beginning in 1853, as superintendent of Indian affairs. During a three-year period of hopelessly bitter conflict, particularly in the war-torn Rogue River Valley of southwestern Oregon, Palmer distinguished himself as a fair-minded superintendent who passionately sought peace. Though certainly not immune to the notorious ethnocentrism of his era, Palmer possessed an unusual sense of justice, embracing Indians' rights as well as whites.' Partly as an emergency measure to protect Indians from the growing numbers of whites who called for their extermination, Palmer initiated the reservation system in Oregon. While this strategy by no means solved what was essentially an insoluble problem, it was perhaps the most notable act of Palmer's superintendency.

In the end, it was Joel Palmer's sympathy with the plight of the Indians that largely caused his undoing as superintendent of Indian affairs. Despite his success persuading the Indians to cede large portions of their land, Palmer grew increasingly unpopular among whites for his pursuit of peace and compromise, and he was dismissed from office in 1856. During his remaining years in Oregon Palmer failed in a number of business enterprises and succeeded in making a political comeback, first as Oregon's Speaker of the House, and later as a state senator. He died in 1881 at the age of seventy.

1810   Born October 4 in Elizabethtown, Canada, to Quakers Ephraim and Anna Palmer.

1822   Bound out (a form of indentured service) for four years in the Catskills, New York. During this time, Palmer received three months of schooling—the only formal education he ever had.

1826   Moved to Philadelphia, Pennsylvania, and took work on a canal project.

1836   Married Sarah Ann Derbyshire, also a Quaker, of Philadelphia. Moved to Laurel, Indiana, near the Ohio River.

1843   Elected to the Indiana state legislature as a Democrat. Re-elected one year later for a second term.

1845   First journey on the Oregon Trail.

1846   Returned to Indiana (in the United States) to fetch his family for a permanent move back to the Oregon County.

1847 Published *Journal of Travels Over the Rocky Mountains, 1845-1846.*
(In addition to recounting Palmer's experiences of 1845-46 on the Oregon
Trail, *Journal of Travels* contains a detailed description of the Willamette
Valley, the Oregon Coast, and the lower Columbia River at that time.)
Returned to Oregon to settle with his family.

Appointed, in December, by Oregon's provisional government to serve
in the Cayuse Indian War as commissary general; hence the nickname
"General" Joel Palmer. Served for the war's six-month duration and
participated in peace negotiations.

1848 Joined the rush to California for gold and returned the following spring,
having made two thousand dollars. Historians estimate that some two-
thirds of Oregon's men went to California during this time.

1850 Helped found the town of Dayton, Oregon, near his Yamhill River land
claim.

1853 Appointed superintendent of Indian affairs for the Oregon Territory by
President Franklin Pierce. Served for three years.

1862 Elected to the Oregon legislature—and in turn chosen as Speaker of the
House—as a member of the recently created Republican party, which
had absorbed both Whigs and anti-slavery Democrats like Palmer.

1864 Elected to the Oregon state senate.

1866 Nominated by the Republican party caucus to represent Oregon in the
U.S. Senate (before U.S. Senators were elected by popular vote). Palmer
refused the nomination, citing a clause in the state constitution that
forbade the holding of two offices at once.

1870 Nominated a Republican party candidate for governor. He lost by a mere
631 votes. Palmer's contemporary, Timothy Davenport, called the defeat

"an opportunity for those of his fellow citizens who thought him too kind to the Indians, to register their disapproval."

1871   Appointed Indian Agent at Siletz Indian Reservation on the Oregon coast. Palmer resigned in November of 1872, "disheartened and utterly discouraged in this work."

1881   Joel Palmer died on 9 June in Dayton, Oregon, after a period of illness and decline.